Angelica is lone⸺ ⸺ed house
in the country. ⸺ busy writing his books,
her mother has gone away and they never see her.

Then (did the house help?) she finds the diary written
by Alex more than fifty years earlier. It is like having
a friend to stay in the house who knows things to do
and places to go, secrets of all sorts, though there's
one secret that even Alex won't tell. Because of Alex,
Angelica gets to know more and more people, exciting
things happen and when she and her father decide
to hold a house-having party, the house is full of
friends.

Barbara Giles

Alex is My Friend

Published with the assistance of
The Literature Board of the Australia Council

Puffin Books

Puffin Books, Penguin Books Australia Ltd,
487 Maroondah Highway, P.O. Box 257
Ringwood, Victoria, 3134, Australia
Penguin Books Ltd,
Harmondsworth, Middlesex, England
Penguin Books,
40 West 23rd Street, New York, N.Y. 10010, U.S.A.
Penguin Books Canada Ltd,
2801 John Street, Markham, Ontario, Canada,
Penguin Books (N.Z.) Ltd,
182-190 Wairau Road, Auckland 10, New Zealand

First published by Penguin Books Australia, 1984

Copyright © Barbara Giles, 1984

Typeset in Cloister Light by
Dovatype, Melbourne

Made and printed in Hong Kong by
LP & Associates

CIP

Giles, Barbara.
Alex is my friend.

For children.
ISBN 0 14 031673 6.

I. Title.

A823'.3

For Faby, Ishmael, David and Robin

Contents

Contents

1

House All Alone

A sad, empty house, it stood all alone among high, blue hills. There were no other houses for miles and miles.

When Mrs Dalloway lived there, the house was happy. The garden was full of flowers, smoke rose from the chimneys and a small red car stood in the garage, ready to go to town at any moment.

You could hear music, and voices. People came to stay, for hours, for a week, for a month.

It didn't matter then that there were no other houses to be seen, that those high blue hills shut off the view.

But Mrs Dalloway grew old. She went to the other side of the world, to live with her son in Atlanta, Georgia, U.S.A.

'You must let my house to a nice family,' she said to Mr Blackmore, the agent. 'Don't make the rent too high. I just want my house to be loved.'

'It won't be easy,' he said. 'It's a long way from anywhere.'

'It's a wonderful house,' said Mrs Dalloway. 'I'm sure you'll find someone.'

She began to pack up her books and boxes to take with her, and one morning the little red car left the house for the last time.

Mrs Dalloway drove off to the airport for her long journey across the world to Atlanta.

The house looked glum.

There was no smoke at the chimneys, no one looked after the flowers, weeds began to choke the beds.

The grass was cut sometimes, but no one cut the dead roses. No one swept the leaves from the porch. Apples fell off the trees, went brown and shrivelled. In the winter no bonfires ate up the rubbish.

There were rabbits in the garden, and a fox came to hunt.

No one seemed to want the house; people came to look, but it was too big, too small, too far away.

'My wife doesn't care for it.'

'The children would have miles to go to school.'

'But,' Mr Blackmore would say, 'it has the phone and Porta gas . . .'

'No, no,' they'd interrupt, 'this won't do.'

He did manage to let it once, but they were terrible people, and he was glad when they went away.

Two years went by and then . . .

On a sunny day in June Angelica and her father came to see the house, all alone in its wild garden, empty and sad.

But on that bright June day the house seemed to be smiling.

This house is pleased to see us, Angelica thought. It wants company.

Mr Blackmore showed them everything. He somehow guessed that Mr Scott was the right man for the house. Angelica followed them through the rooms. She stared silently. Mr Blackmore tried to talk to her, but he wasn't very good with children. Still, he tried.

'I want space for a studio,' said Mr Scott. 'This big front bedroom looks right for that, lots of light.

And this small one next to it will do for my writing room.

'I write stories for children and I do the pictures too. We don't need five bedrooms, Angelica and I. Just one each, and one for a visitor. We'll clear most of the furniture out of here and stack it somewhere else. And I'll roll up the carpet so it won't get painty.

'I think it will do us very nicely, if we can get someone to come and clean for us now and then.'

'No trouble about that,' said Mr Blackmore. He was so pleased the house was let he'd have promised anything, but his Mrs Wright turned out to be as good as her name.

They moved in and the house got warm from attic to cellar. There were no attics, but that was what Mrs Wright said. 'It's a grand old house and it will soon be warm from attic to cellar.'

It was warm, but it was rather quiet. Mr Scott worked hard and Angelica had lessons to do from the correspondence school.

Angie and her father got on fine together. Mr Scott did the cooking, Angelica set the table and cleared up. They had a dishwasher, so nobody had to worry about whose-turn-to-do-the-dishes.

Mr Scott was a very good cook. He made

omelettes, pizzas, pies and roast chicken. 'Plate-lickin' good,' said Angelica. 'All your cooking is plate-lickin' good.'

She was good at doing a boiled fruit cake, which wasn't a cake boiled, but you boiled up everything together and *then* baked it. It was delicious; she got the recipe off the fruit packet.

On sunny days they barbecued sausages and steak. Mr Scott found an old oven shelf at the back of the shed, and built it up on bricks. It worked fine.

The scraps went to the birds. They had no idea a rat family came and got their share, until one day they saw the stout grandfather rat come out of the bushes and scuttle back in again.

'Aha,' said Mr Scott, 'that looks like a reason for a dog. Do we need a reason for a dog, Angelica, angel?'

'We need a dog for a reason,' she said.

'And what's the reason?'

'For company,' said Angelica.

He looked at her and said, 'Missing Mum?'

For Angelica's mother, who was of course Mr Scott's wife, had gone away quite suddenly. She had only written three times, and the last time was back in the summer.

It looked as if she meant to stay away.

The very next day they went to town and talked to people about a dog. The man in the newsagent's seemed to know the most. He sent them down the coast road to a place called Robin's Nest. There they looked after dogs for people who had to go away. The man had dogs of his own and puppies for sale. They looked at the pups. They were fox terriers.

'Keep the rats away, these fellows. Very sharp.'

'Useful,' said Mr Scott. 'But I really want a dog that will be a friend for my daughter.'

'He'll be a friend, your foxy, if you make a friend of him,' said the Robin's Nest man. 'How about this little fellow? Look at the cute spot over his eye. And you can have these chaps inside the house, you know, because they don't leave their hairs around.'

'Oh, please yes,' said Angelica, 'and we'll give him a basket in the kitchen. It's too cold outside for a baby.'

'Give him a hot water bottle inside his cushion for the first few nights,' said the man. 'They often cry at first. Miss the others, miss being all curled up together.'

So they took Spot home, and he did cry a bit the first night. On the second night, Angie gave him a little clock to listen to. She had read about that in a book.

He didn't cry any more, though it mightn't have been the clock. Spot soon learnt his name and when he stopped being so fat, he learnt to sit up and beg and jump a stick and to sit when told. He was really a very satisfactory dog and good company.

At night, when they sat in front of the fire, Spot was there to talk to if her father went into a dream about a new story. Spot even got into the book, about seven children and a dog; he sat very still while Mr Scott drew him and Angelica together.

The girls in the book were all Angelica, only one had red hair, one was blonde and one had brown curls, which made them look different. For Angelica had long straight hair, as black as the blackest thing you can think of – coal, perhaps – and eyes to match.

He wasn't getting the boys right, somehow, and he said, 'We'll have to get Toby up for a week, I can't seem to draw these boys properly just out of my head.'

'What will you do when Toby and I get too big for your books?' said Angelica. 'Move into town? Adopt some children?' She wasn't keen on the idea of Toby coming to stay, even though she was still a bit lonely. But it would be great to see Aunt Janet. She was fun.

Toby was still Toby.

'What's this you've got, this little black and white runt? Call that a dog? You should have a big dog that's good for something. A Saint Bernard. An Alsatian. A Dalmatian. A little yapping fox terrier! Nobody has fox terriers now.'

'Well, I do,' said Angie, 'and he doesn't yap.'

Toby began to annoy Spot.

'Got no spirit, the little rabbit,' he said when Spot just ran off to his hidey-hole.

'Don't bother that dog,' said Aunt Janet. 'It was quite happy till you disturbed it.'

How could Aunt Janet have such a bothersome boy? Angelica could never make it out. Perhaps he was like his father, who was mostly in other countries writing news about wars and floods, so that nobody really got to know him. Toby certainly wasn't like his mum.

But he was a good model. He didn't mind sitting still, he didn't mind running and jumping to order. He liked being in the books.

'But it only makes him more pleased with himself than ever,' said Angelica to her father after they had gone.

'Keeps him out of his mother's way for a bit,'

he said. 'I don't think she likes him very much.'

A mother not to like her child! That was a new idea for Angie. Yet Mum had not come back. She felt sad again.

It was the end of the winter, which often seems to be the worst. It was cold and windy and wet; really the weather was not one bit helpful to a girl who had no one to play with.

'Spot, I can play with you, and it's fun, dear little dog. But you don't talk.'

Her father was very busy, finishing off the pictures for the book about the seven children.

Seven children, she thought, and I haven't anyone. She didn't even have schoolwork due. It was supposed to be the holidays. She had read all her books, more than once.

She sat and stared out at the driving rain. The wind was tossing the weeping willow about and bending the tops of the tall trees.

Weeping willow. That was her. What was she to do? She went into her father's study to practise on the typewriter. Soon she was going to send all her lessons to the correspondence school in type.

No more nasty remarks like 'Care must be taken with writing. You cannot expect to get full marks if we cannot read your work'.

2

Open the Door

The weather seemed to be getting worse. The house shook in a sudden gust of wind. They say 'safe as houses', thought Angelica, but you'd think we were going to blow away any minute.

She stopped typing to put in a fresh sheet of paper. Then she looked at the wall in front of her and thought what to do next. It was a pretty wallpaper, rosebuds. Not right for a study, but of course this was meant to be a bedroom. Upstairs always was.

She went on typing. 'The quick brown fox jumps over the lazy dog.' All the letters of the

alphabet. She was getting better, she wasn't looking at the keys at all. Only at the rosebuds.

The house shook again in the wind. And in the
wall, right in front of her eyes, a crack opened up
in the wallpaper. A crack in the shape of a door.

Spot got up from the rug where he had been
asleep, and went to the wall and sniffed.

'What's there, Spot?' said Angelica. 'Rats?'
Spot went and sat down again. So it wasn't rats.

She got up for a closer look. A little cold air
came through the crack. The door was not really
door-size, more like a cupboard. She pulled out
the desk and pushed. Nothing happened.

Locked. It must be locked. She felt down the
sides about where she thought a catch should be.

Suddenly the door went in. Doors don't usually
go *in* to cupboards. There was light in there, too.

She stepped through the doorway. The light
came from a window in the roof. Very dim on this
damp, dark day. But enough to see that all there
was in the room was an old-fashioned desk, a chair
and bookshelves.

And a photograph of an old lady and a child
on the wall. She wiped the dust off it with her
handkerchief. The child was dressed like
Angelica's grandmother in the only photograph
they had of her when she was small. A cotton frock
with the waist cut low, hair short with a fringe. She

was standing on a beach in the sun with a woman who wore a rather long dress and a cardigan. She had her hair cut short, too, with a slide that held it across her forehead and to one side They were laughing.

They held a string of fish between them. There was writing on the photograph; it was hard to make out, but it seemed to be 'Gamma and Alex, 1928'.

Everything was thick with dust. The wallpaper was rosebuds, though not the same rosebuds as next door in the study. Even the paper was dusty.

Angelica went and fetched a duster, a dustpan and a broom. She didn't know where to start, so she swept the desk and the chair and the bookcase, and then the floor, and did a quick job with the duster.

'I'll do it properly tomorrow,' she said. 'Right now I want to look at those books.'

There were books she had herself, like *Alice in Wonderland, At the Back of the North Wind* and *The Secret Garden.*

There were books that looked older, with gold on their covers and the edges of the leaves.

In some of them was the name 'Maie Mitchell', and in the oldest ones, 'Violet Helen Kelsall, her book' in fancy writing with curly capital letters. Most of them belonged to Alex Dalloway. 'Alex, with love from Mother', 'Christmas Greetings to Alex, 1929', 'Alex from Gamma'.

She dusted the books and picked out three to read after tea. She chose *A Little Bush Maid, A Thorny Path*, which had very sad pictures, and *Reggie, Queenie and Blot* which seemed to be about India.

Then she shut the door and smoothed the paper over the crack. She wanted to give her father a surprise.

She went downstairs to set the table.

After tea, when the dishwasher was washing up, she settled down to read, and pretended not to see her father looking at the books. She made herself snug, legs over the arm of the big chair, and began on *Reggie, Queenie and Blot*. Blot was a foxie like Spot; right away he saved Reggie from a crazy elephant, it was all escapes and disguises.

'I thought you said you were sick of all your books.'

'But these aren't my books.'

'Where did they come from then? Aunt Janet?'

'I found them. In a cupboard.'

Her father picked up *A Thorny Path*. 'This one is very old. A hundred years, I'd say. But where is this cupboard? There were no books here that I remember.'

'Upstairs.'

'Where upstairs?'

'Did you go into your study before tea?'

'Yes.'

'Well, you should have seen the cupboard then.'

'I saw the one I had to buy because there wasn't a cupboard.'

'But there was a cupboard all the time.'

'You're teasing me, Angelica. Come and show me this invisible cupboard.'

When she showed him, he said, 'How did you know where to cut the paper?'

'It wasn't me. Right under my eyes the house opened up that crack. But I found out how to work the catch.' She pressed and the door sprang open.

'See. It isn't really a cupboard, either. It's got a window.'

'I expect it's meant for storing trunks and boxes and things. Could be a bit stuffy. But someone has used it.' He looked at the photograph. 'Gamma and Alex, 1928.'

'Alex must be Mrs Dalloway,' said Angelica.

'No. She's not old enough. Mr Blackmore said Mrs Dalloway was over eighty. And she's not Gamma either. Gamma's too old.'

'Gamma is baby talk for Grandma,' said Angelica.

Mr Scott opened the desk. There were letters

there, and a diary. Inside the cover it said 'Alex Dalloway, 1927', and

Finder be kind, if this book you find.
Don't read what I say till I tell you you may.

'Dad,' said Angelica as he turned the pages of the big red book, 'don't read it. Alex wanted it to be private.'

'You're being silly,' said her father. 'What could it matter now?'

'Dad, please!'

There was a sudden shriek of wind. The lights went out.

There was a great stumbling to get out of the little room and into the study to find matches. They had hardly got downstairs to the fuse box when the lights came on again.

'Temporary interruption of service,' said Mr Scott. But he didn't go upstairs again, and before she went to bed, Angelica hid the red diary behind the books in the little room. She didn't know if her father looked for it, because he never mentioned it again.

Probably he thought Angelica was right, or he didn't want to upset her, or both.

3

A Friend

When Mrs Wright came to clean, Angelica showed her the little room.

'That lino would come up lovely with a scrub and a bit of a polish,' said Mrs Wright. 'Good old stuff, it is. I'll just take up the rough with the vac. first.'

'No, I'll do it,' said Angelica, and she did, and cleaned and polished the furniture too.

Mrs Wright got the stepladder and washed the skylight. She found it opened if you pulled a cord that ran down the wall, so she cleaned the outside too, and the room was lighter at once.

'There's a power point just outside in the study; you can have a lamp and a heater too, love, if you leave the door open. I'll get a little one out from the cupboard under the stairs, and a little mat, too.

'Now you've a place all of your own when your dad is painting his pictures or writing his books.'

Angelica got a cushion, the oldest, from the lounge downstairs and put it on her chair. The room wasn't cold, either, because the living-room chimney came up along one wall which was always warm. Spot decided he'd lie against the chimney on the new mat. 'Spot's spot,' said Angie. She read her way through the books. Some of them were rather dull, but anything was better than sitting watching the rain falling, falling.

You couldn't see a thing outside, and for a few days they couldn't get to town because the creek was in flood, and water was all over the flats this side of the bridge.

Spot came off worst, because he liked only fresh meat.

'It's tinned meat or do without, Spot,' said Mr Scott. But eggs and bacon and tinned ham, powdered milk and soda bread did very well for Angelica and her father.

One of the books she had found was about children cut off from everybody by a flood. It was three hundred years ago, and the children didn't have clean drinking water, let alone tinned meat.

Of course, they were rescued. Children are always rescued in books, thought Angelica, but then she remembered all the children who died in the books that had once belonged to Violet Kelsall. One or more to every book.

She talked to her father about it.

'Children did die more often in those days,' he said, 'so you'd expect them to die in books too. Now we don't have so many children, and most of them grow up. Doctors know so much more now.

'But if you think about it, there are people dying in some books for kids these days. What about that book, *The Moon Tree*, where the child goes in a dream to visit his dead grandparents?'

'Oh, grandparents.' Angelica had never had grandparents that she remembered, so it seemed quite natural to her for grandparents to die.

'As a matter of fact, Angelica, my very next book will be the story of a brave child who is dying, knowing all about it.'

'Is that why you've looked so glum when you've been sitting by the fire? Planning ... ?'

'Partly. And partly because the people who do

my books are going to argue. They'll want him to live.'

'But children do die.'

'Do children read books for fun, or to find things out?'

'Both, I'd say.'

Later she'd remember this conversation and think how strange it was they should have talked like that.

Next day Angie was sitting at the little desk, doing her maths. She was feeling rather tired, and when her father called, 'Nearly lunch time,' she thought she'd stop right away.

She put her maths book down on top of the bookshelves, open at the place she was up to, while she tidied her desk.

Then she went down for lunch. Scrambled eggs with ham, apples and cheese. She felt better after that.

When she went back upstairs, she couldn't find her maths book. She remembered where she had put it. It wasn't there.

The bookshelves didn't pull out, so she pulled out books to find it. There it was, behind the second shelf, astride the hidden diary. She pulled them both out together.

The diary fell open at a page with a drawing of a girl who had long black hair just like Angelica's own. Underneath was written 'My friend Angelica.'

It went on, 'I am writing this for no one else to see but my friend Angelica.

'I only saw you once, Angelica. Or I should say, I only dreamed you once. But I knew at once we should be friends.

'It will be nice to have a friend my age. Gamma and Mother are wonderful. But they know so much, and they forget a bit what being young is like.

'I feel mean, Angelica, when I say this, because they are kind, but if I had just one friend.

'But now I've got you, and I'll tell you everything.'

Angelica forgot about maths. She read on and on.

Soon she began to know Alex well. Alex Dalloway. She had no father, just a mother. Her father had died just after the First World War, before Alex was born. But she had a grandmother. Gamma brought the baby Alex and her young mother from England, to live with her in this big house in the country.

'My father was a hero,' said Alex, 'but he died of it. He died because he was wounded, just before the fighting stopped. He never saw me at all.'

The big house had more people in it then, coming and going all the time. They had a telephone, and Gamma was the first lady to drive a car in that part of Victoria. They had a lot of visitors, they knew what was going on in the world.

Every year they went down to the inlet for a month. They fished, they swam. They had a boat.

But 'they' were all grown up. Except one. There was a boy, Colin. Every year he was down at the inlet before them, waiting. Every year they spent all their time together. They were often with Gamma, sailing.

Mother played golf a lot. She got seasick, so she didn't go out in the boat. 'I get seasick in the bath if I splash too much,' she said one day.

The writing was a bit hard to read. Alex didn't write the way Angie had been taught. And the ink was faded pale brown in places. She hadn't read more than a quarter of the way through when it was tea time.

'Well, Angel, have you finished your school work?' asked her father. 'I have to go to town

21

tomorrow, and then I shan't be in for a week. We must get it in the post.'

Angelica looked guilty. 'I've been reading. I'll hurry up with the rest in the morning. I'll set my alarm and get up early.'

'As long as you're ready by eleven. OK?'

'Yes,' she said, 'I'll be ready.'

The next day they set off for their eighty kilometre drive to town. Alex and her people used to stay the night sometimes. The Scotts never had. Yet.

4

Ups and Downs

It had been dark over the mountains all afternoon. When they had finished their shopping, which included a new red jumper and jeans for each of them – 'the father and daughter look,' said her dad – it was raining hard. They got quite wet just running to the car park.

When they reached the river crossing, the marker showed nearly a metre of water over the road. 'We'll wait a bit, it might go down,' said Mr Scott.

But it went up. A metre and a half, two metres. They had to back away from the flood.

'Let's go back to town and have some tea.'

They had dinner at the hotel. Angelica enjoyed her apple pie with cream. Dad didn't usually bother to cook sweets.

The hotel lady said, 'So you're stuck in town, Mr Scott. A flash flood. But it's not going to stop raining, you know. Just listen to that on the roof. Regular cloud burst.

'Better let me book you in for the night.

'There's TV in the lounge, if you want to watch. And the papers.'

The TV was all snow because of the storm. Angie fiddled with it, but it was no good. Then she tried the piano, then she wandered about the room. It surely was raining hard. And blowing like anything.

Dad just sat and read the paper. There was no one else around.

A tall girl with copper plaits put her head in the door.

'I'm Helen. Mum told me you were here. Like to play table tennis?'

'I'll be terrible. I haven't played for ages.'

'So will I,' said Helen. 'Come on, then.'

They were both pretty bad. 'I don't often have anyone to play with,' Helen said. 'Mostly the people with kids stay at the Motel.'

'What's it like, living in a hotel?' Angie asked.

'A house has *got* to be better. Mum's always busy. And some of my friends aren't allowed to come here by their parents.

'Still, could be worse. I've lots of friends in town, and the pool's just around the corner.'

She caught Angie way off balance with a lightning return.

They played till Dad came looking for them. 'How's it going?' he asked.

'A bit of practice and we'd both be stars,' said Helen.

'But now, bed,' he said. 'I'm ready for it, Angie, and you'd better be. It's stopped raining. We'll be able to get off in the morning, I'd think.'

'There's electric blankets,' said Helen's mother when they met her in the passage. 'Sleep tight.'

Angie slept till nearly nine, when Dad woke her. Helen had gone to school when they went down to breakfast. The morning was clear and bright.

'I liked Helen,' said Angie as she dripped honey on a second slice of toast. 'I wish she lived nearer.'

'Well, she can visit,' said Dad. 'River's down again, I had a look at it earlier.'

So they set off once more. This time they had a passenger, a man who was going to the forestry camp, a few kilometres beyond their house.

All the way, he talked to Mr Scott about re-planting the forests. 'Forests,' he said, 'stop flash floods like that one last night. Take up the water like a sponge.

'Lucky to be alive, I am. Just reached that bridge when down came this great wall of water, carried off me and the bike.

'I was lucky to fetch up in the arms of a tree. They found the old bike down river this morning. I don't think it will ever work again.'

Dad and the forestry man – 'I'm Joe,' he said – went on talking about bare mountains that used to be forests, about landslides, about forests cut down to build ships or to clear the land for farming.

Angelica was only half listening. She was thinking about the diary and how she must reach the end.

When they were near the house, her father said, 'We've got to take Joe to the camp.'

'Can't I get out, Dad? Mrs Wright's here, I can see her car.'

Spot came racing down the drive, full of jumps and barks of joy to see her.

Angie went in and said 'Hello' to Mrs Wright, and then ran upstairs. There was the diary; she picked it up and began to read where she had left off.

But the temptation was too much. She knew the diary ended before all the pages had been used up. Why did Alex stop?

Had she just got tired of it? If she had known that someday a real live Angelica would read it, would she have gone on?

She turned the leaves till she came to the last page of writing.

It just stopped. The last date was December the twentieth: 'Busy, busy. Going tomorrow. What fun to see Colin.'

Why had Alex stopped writing? Oh well, people do. She had kept a diary once herself, for six months. And stopped. She had no idea where it was now. Perhaps Alex had found a real friend. Or just become bored. Or gone away to school.

She could hear her father downstairs singing a song about winter as he got the lunch. She must go down.

Later she would read the rest of Alex's diary.

At lunch her father said, 'I found out all about your Alex and Maie and Violet, talking to Mrs Casey at the hotel.'

'I know about them,' said Angelica.

'You know! How did you find out? You haven't been talking to anyone but the cleaning lady, and

27

she's new here, Mrs. . . I always forget her name. Fazackerly, isn't it?'

'Wright, said Angelica. 'No. No one told me.'

'You read the diary then. That's a change of mind.'

'I read the diary. The house wanted me to.'

'Angelica! How can you say anything so daft!'

'It did. In any case, it's addressed to me.'

'Addressed to everybody! What was it? "Don't read what I say till I tell you you may." How could you get past that?'

'The house opened the door. And the book. And the diary begins "Dear Angelica".'

'Angelica who? She'd be sixty by now if she was Alex's age.'

'Angelica, the friend she wanted.'

She had had enough of this. She began to cry. 'She was lonely on her own, Dad. Like me.'

'Angel.' He put his arm round her. 'I've been working too hard, I haven't spent enough time with you lately. And only that awful Toby to stay for the holidays.

'I'll tell you what we'll do. You get your school work done as far ahead as you can. And if you don't finish, I'll write a note. And we'll go up north, where it will be warmer. We might even be able to swim.

'Spot? Oh he can stay at Robin's Nest.'

5
Winter Sun

Two days after that, they caught a plane north. And another plane. Then there was a car ride, and then . . .

A tiny bay with rocks at each end. Only three houses, each with its own steps down to the beach. There was a little jetty with a boat moored, and a boathouse.

Dad stopped the car he had hired at the airport outside the largest of the houses, and went up the steps to the door.

'Mr Scott,' said the woman who opened it. 'Come from down south to get away from the cold and the wet?

'That's your cottage, the green one. And you can get anything you want from me. Even fishing lines and bait. I put milk and eggs and stuff like that in your fridge. How was it down south? I come from Tassie meself, used to get snow in the winter there, 'course we was high up ...'

She seemed as though she'd go on talking a long time, so Dad said, 'You must excuse us, we're tired and hungry.'

'Anything I can do just ask.' She gave them the key.

'Lunch, a sleep and a swim,' said Dad when they got inside their cottage.

Lunch was boiled eggs and crusty fresh bread with butter, strawberry milk – there was a carton in the fridge – and apples.

'Did you know that they grow apples in Queensland? Up high, where it's cooler?'

Angela just smiled to show that she had heard. They had left home at five a.m. to drive to the town and on to the airport. She was dead tired.

And they'd changed planes in Sydney, and waited around for ages. Now for a snooze, and that swim later.

That was a wonderful fortnight.

Every morning they swam before breakfast. Out of their door, down the steps, and into the water.

Most days they just stayed in their bathers all day. They pottered round the bay in the little boat and fished. They went on trips in the car. Once up to the mountains, and on the way back, to an aquarium, full of tropical fish in fancy dress. To another place where they went out in a glass-bottomed boat to see coral growing. Fancy fishes there too, swimming free in water like glass.

The second week a family came to stay in the empty house.

They came in the late afternoon, trailing a boat behind their car. There was another boat, a quite small one, on the roof rack of their station wagon.

Angel and her father had just come in, they were having a snack in the kitchen.

'Sailing people,' said Mr Scott. She thought of Alex and Gamma.

There were two children in the family tumbling out of the wagon, a small girl and a boy about her own age, or a bit older perhaps. They began unloading.

Mrs Maggs was there in two shakes of a lamb's tail, giving them her line about 'Come to get away from the cold and wet', and holding on to the key of the house till they had to ask for it.

She went back to her cottage in no great hurry,

after watching them unload. She quizzed the kids about their names and ages, but Angie couldn't quite hear the answers. Dad said, 'That woman's lonely.'

'They look nice,' she said. 'I wonder if they'll stay long?'

They were staying a week. The children came out after tea and walked along the beach. They called 'Hi!' to Angie as they passed, then went on walking towards the near point where the rocks had tumbled down from the cliff. The tide was too high to get around into Sugar Bay and they turned back. Angie sat down on the porch and picked up her book so as not to be staring when they passed.

They stopped in front of the house, and leaned on the fence.

'Hello,' said the little girl. 'What's your name? I'm Sue. This is Andy, my brother. He's twelve almost.'

'Angie Scott. Welcome to Treacle Bay.'

'What's around the point?' said the boy.

'Just another bay, but not as nice as ours. More houses. And shops.'

'We are going sailing tomorrow,' said Sue.

'Perhaps,' said Andy. 'At least I'll get the Sabot in the water.'

There was a call from the end house. 'Coming,' said Andy.

Angelica went inside. 'Why don't we use the sail on that boat of ours instead of the outboard?' she said.

'Because I can't sail,' said her dad.

'Andy could teach you,' said Angelica.

'And who's Andy, my sail-struck child? One of the experts who've just arrived?'

Angelica sniffed. 'What's wrong with learning something new?'

It was still early when she woke in the morning. She sat straight up and looked out of the window at the bay.

There was Andy in the little yellow and white boat she'd seen stacked on the car roof. Morning wind filled the sail, the water was almost too bright to look at. Each little dancing wave threw back a silver edge of light.

She got up and into her swim suit. When she reached the water's edge the boat was already coming back to shore. Andy jumped out in the shallows, and she helped him pull the boat in till it grounded on the sand.

Another heave and 'Thanks, she'll be all right now,' said Andy. 'Gosh, I want my breakfast. See you later,' and he made off for their house. There was a smell of frying bacon on the air, and after the shortest morning swim yet, Angie went in.

'Dad,' she said as he turned the bacon, 'Andy could sail our boat.'

'So you said last night, Angelica. I'll stick to the old putt-putt. Today we might go round to the far point, to that bay we haven't fished yet.'

'The Bellamys are going sailing.'

'The Bellamys! Why this craze for sailing, Miss Scott?'

'Alex sailed,' said Angie.

'Alex did? Well you shall sail too. I'm sure young Andy will take you out. Quit worrying. All things come round to those who wait.'

The Bellamys showed no sign of going sailing that morning. They unhitched the boat trailer and turned the station wagon round. They lowered the mast on Andy's boat, and removed the rudder. Then they carried her up the beach above the high tide mark.

Mr Scott went over and introduced himself. 'Not sailing weather?' he asked.

'Not really, not for our *Nautilus*. She's not really an ocean-going boat. There's a bit of wind blowing up, it could be pretty rough. We're going to picnic inland, and pick up a bit of shopping, go to the laundrette, all that sort of thing.'

Angelica looked glum, and she was glum all afternoon, for it was too rough for them to go fishing to Vinegar Bay. Later on, it began to rain a little. She sat by the window with a book, watching for the Bellamys.

They came home in the late afternoon. Andy and Sue came over right away.

'Mum says don't start cooking if you like crab. Come about seven and eat with us. Stay the evening. See ya.' They raced off.

'Angie, your face looks quite different. Do you really like crab that much?' said her father, laughing.

The crab was beaut. Everyone ate and talked nonstop.

The Bellamys had been further north, to a sailing contest for juniors. 'Andy's going to compete in the national Sabot championships this summer. We wanted him to get in a bit of practice. The weather hasn't been much down our way for sailing.'

'Down our way' was the Gippsland lakes, where they had their weekend house.

'Bedtime for us, Angelica,' said Dad. But Mr Bellamy said he wanted supper, so it was twelve when they left.

A different day entirely, then. The morning bright and sunny with a light wind. Angie was up early as early.

But there was no sign of Andy till after breakfast. Then he came out with his father, and Sue trailing behind. The kids were carrying their life jackets. Lucky Sue, thought Angelica.

They got *Dolphin* down to the water. She looked like a huge saucer, lying on her side. They stepped the mast, fitted the boom and sail, and fixed the rudder. Angie tried to remember everything they did.

Then they pushed her off into the water. Andy, holding the tiller, tumbled aboard, shoved down the centreboard and turned *Dolphin* till she caught the wind. Suddenly the sail filled, and she wasn't a saucer with a sail, but a bird skimming across the bay.

Mr Scott came down from the house. 'How long's he been sailing?' he asked.

'Since he was seven or thereabouts. Of course he'd watched us working *Princess*, that's the boat we had before *Nautilus*, since he wasn't much more than a baby. They learn a lot just watching.

'And they learn fast on their own, pottering around, getting the feel of a boat, discovering how to move it with sail and oars.'

'It must be fun,' said Angie, 'to have your own boat.'

'You'd like to be out there with him, eh, Angie? Well, that's Andy's boat, and it's not often he takes anyone out in it, he's very serious about his sailing. Even Sue has to wait till she's asked, though he's promised to take her out this morning.

'But we'll take you sailing in *Nautilus* tomorrow, if we can borrow you from your father. We plan to drive down to Mirabel Waters tomorrow and sail all day.'

'Great!' said Angie, jumping for joy. 'If you don't mind, Dad.'

Sue came bouncing up and dragged Angie away to look at a baby octopus she'd found washed up.

'Angelica's fascinated,' said her father. 'Some of it is because of somebody she knows.' He stopped. Could you talk about Alex like that?

'Yes, they like to measure up to someone else. But this isn't the place for her to learn, this open bay. Boats are much safer than they used to be, but you need to know what you're doing in a place like this.

'You ought to come down before summer ends to our place on the lakes and stay a while. It's shallow near us, safe as houses, sheltered from the wind. Just the place for a child to learn.'

'Thank you. We might do just that.'

6
Sailing

Mirabel Waters was a fantastic place, all sky and bright water. They drove right on to the shore of the lake and backed the trailer down to the edge. *Nautilus* slipped gently off, and floated.

'Hold her, Andy,' said Mr Bellamy. They scrambled aboard with lunch baskets and all their gear, while he moved the car up the beach.

'Life jackets?' he checked.

'Sunscreen, anyone?' said Mrs Bellamy, dabbing Sue's back.

They were away, with a good wind. The lake

shores unwound; sails of many colours dotted the blue water.

Angelica found out what gybing meant, she learnt to duck the boom when 'Gybe-oh' was called and the sails swung over. She discovered why the crew lean out in a strong wind, balancing the boat.

They saw one boat go over and watched while her crew righted her. One man stood on the centreboard and pulled, the other moved round to grab the tiller. In no time they were aboard, bailing out the water, and ready to sail again. 'Smart work,' said Andy.

They told her rope names, 'Though they aren't usually called ropes,' they explained. Sheets and halyards were for hauling on – they were attached to the sails; the painter was what you used to tie the boat to the jetty or a convenient post.

She listened to the sounds of a boat, the clink-ing of fittings, the rush of water, the thap and whack of sails. She even helped a bit, though mostly she just watched and remembered.

They got home at dusk.

'Had a good day?' said her father. 'Sunburnt?'

'Yes,' said Angie, 'and no. Gosh, Dad, I'm tired.'

She slept without waking, without dreaming even.

Andy came to the kitchen door as they were finishing breakfast.

'Hi, Angie,' he said. 'Like to go sailing?'

Would she like to! She called to Dad, and ran.

Dolphin was rigged and ready. They floated her. Andy told her to hold the tiller while he scrambled in. They didn't talk much, except for Andy saying 'Hike out' when the boat heeled, and 'Better bail her out a bit' or 'You're catching on.'

She felt at home in tiny *Dolphin*, empty but for bailer and paddle. 'The law says you must have those, and tied on,' said Andy, 'in case it's flat calm, or you bottle.'

'Bottle?' said Angie.

'Capsize. Move over, slow coach,' said Andy.

But when they came in, he said, 'You're doing all right. When you come down south, you can sail *Dolphin*, right?'

Right! It would be bliss, thought Angelica.

The rest of the week went lightning fast. Fires on the beach after dark, roasting potatoes and grilling sausages on sticks, singing to Mother Bellamy's guitar. Swimming, more swimming, sailing and more sailing; the weather was warm as summer back home.

She was sad when the Bellamys left, but she

knew they'd all be together again at the end of January. Then she'd learn to sail *Dolphin.*

A Sabot, they called the boat, and laughed when she said, 'She isn't wooden and she's not much like a shoe.'

'Class name,' they said, 'and more like a shoe than most. She's plywood under all that shiny paint. Light to move, and one person can sail her.'

They helped the Bellamys load up and leave with 'See you soons' and 'Don't forgets'. Then they went for a last walk in the evening low tide, round the cliffs to Vinegar Bay. 'Such funny names,' said Angie. And when they got home there was Mrs Maggs talking to some new people.

They were Queenslanders, so they didn't get the 'Come up north to get away from' bit. It was 'Welcome to Treacle Bay. Real strange names the bays have got, Sugar, Vinegar and Treacle, but they reckon a ship was lost here with a cargo of them things. The story goes the sea around here was pretty ripe for a while – probably nothing in it . . . Oh, you want your key, and here I am holding on to it.'

'We should have asked Mrs M. down to one of our beach parties, she'd have told us some tales,' said Mr Scott.

'She's not on her own,' Angie said. 'Andy told me Mr Maggs is in the house all right, but he only comes out at night, late. He's a bit odd. Never speaks.'

'And she's lonely,' said her father, 'that's why she talks so much. Poor soul,' and when they were leaving he was extra nice to her and promised they'd tell all their friends about Treacle Bay.

Their last breakfast. They were eating on the porch, saying good-bye to a bay full of morning sunlight.

'Would you like us to live in the north for always?' said Dad. 'I could work anywhere, you know.'

'Could Mum find us if we keep moving around? If she wants to.'

'No worries there. There's Aunt Janet, the people who do my books, oh, lots of people would know where we are.'

Angelica thought a while. 'No, I don't think so, really. Our house is a real house, it feels like a home. I think I like it best.'

'I'm glad about that,' said Dad. 'When we get back we'll try and buy it from Mrs Dalloway. We'll put in a swimming pool for the summer. We'll turn the room over the garage into a bunkroom.

'We'll ask, oh, dozens of people to come and stay. We'll mend the terrace and tidy the garden.

We'll have that girl from the hotel out to stay weekends, if you like. We'll go skiing, looking for gold. And have a huge party for my thirty-ninth birthday.'

Angelica laughed. 'We'll see.'

'You sound like a parent,' he said. 'Well, I'm not going to work quite so hard any more.'

7

Little Secrets

Car, plane. Plane, car.

And there was the house in its trees.

'Has it got a name, this house?' Angelica asked.

'Yes, Kelsall Cottage.'

'Ugh. No wonder no one calls it by its name.'

'If I buy it, you can name it again.'

The house looked pleased to see them. The fruit trees were in blossom, the jonquils in flower. Mrs Wright had been in and tidied.

'Scrambled eggs for lunch, I'll make them,' said Angelica.

It was nearer tea time than lunch time really.

She cooked the eggs slowly, in the pan that didn't stick, with some milk and butter and pepper and salt. And lots of hot toast with butter.

'Mmm, that was good,' said Dad. 'I was starving.'

Mrs Wright rang then to see if they were back. 'And I've got your Spot here,' she said. 'He wasn't too happy at Robin's Nest. Was he glad to see me! No trouble with him at all here. Pick him up when you're ready.'

They had to go shopping in Helicon, so that would be all right. Spot could come home tomorrow.

'We'll need a fire tonight,' Dad said when they had stacked the dishwasher. He went out to get wood, but wandered round the garden, pulling out weeds here and there.

Angelica went up to her hidey-hole.

'Safe back, Alex,' she said.

Then she picked up the diary and began to write where Alex had left off.

'Oh Alex, we went sailing,' she began, and told her about the holidays, about their new friends, Andy, everything. Then she turned back to the place where she had stopped reading before they went away. More than halfway, now. She wanted to read it all, she wanted to make it last.

'Each time I write to you, Alex, I'll read a bit, a page or two.'

Today it was all about Colin coming to stay in September.

'That's right now!' said Angelica.

'After the winter,' Alex said, 'there are often gemstones in the creek behind the house. At the bend where the big willow is.'

Colin had found a garnet, and she'd found a piece of rose quartz.

That night Angelica said to her father, 'Alex says there are gemstones in the creek. And there was this book in her bookcase.'

They looked at it: *How to Find Gemstones.* Sure enough, it said 'Garnets, rock crystal, sapphire, topaz, ruby and very occasionally diamonds, in the creeks of this area.'

There was a chapter on how to find the stones. A bent piece of iron to scrape out holes in the rocks and a sieve to wash the gravel were all you needed.

'And then to pick out the diamonds! I know where the sieve is. Hanging up in the shed behind the garage,' said Angelica. 'Can I have Helen out this weekend? To help look.'

So Helen came to stay the weekend.

On Saturday, right after breakfast, they went to the creek. The water was cold. They wore rubber boots with their jeans tucked in. They poked their hands into holes in the rocks, they scraped with their pieces of bent iron, deep down.

Nothing that looked one bit interesting.

They dug up gravel and washed it in the sieve.

They got very wet.

Finally Helen fell in full length, and when she heard Angelica laughing she pulled her in too.

It was too cold to stay in wet things, so they went back to the house, with a few unsparkly stones in the sieve.

It was lunch time, they were surprised to find. They changed quickly.

After lunch, Mr Scott said, 'Now for the diamonds.'

He poked about with a pair of tweezers. 'You have some little jasper pebbles which would polish very nicely. What's this. A garnet.'

'It's too little to be any use,' said Helen, looking at the tiny red stone.

'Maybe, but nice to have. Why don't you put your jasper and this huge garnet in a jar till next time? When it's a bit warmer, and the creek is low, I'll come out and help you. We'll dig up tonnes of gravel. Sure to find something between us.'

'And I know who we can ask to polish them for

us,' said Helen, 'Mr Palmer, who teaches sixth grade. He has a tumbler that makes them shiny as shiny. They go round and round fast and bump each other smooth.'

After that, Mr Scott got quite used to Angelica rushing downstairs saying 'Alex says this', 'Alex says that'.

'Alex says there is an old hut up the hill where there are scads of daffodils.'

'Alex says there is a secret hiding place in the trunk of the big cedar on the lawn. She put a little box in there for me.'

Her father would sometimes say 'Remember, that's fifty years ago,' but it mostly turned out just like Alex had said. Though the box for Angelica was gone – some climbing child had found it, per- haps – the daffodils were there, and the hut all tumbled down. And there was the little bag of gemstones in the secret drawer of the writing desk, which Angelica would never have found without the help of Alex.

It was almost like having her there, to show all the secret and scary and interesting things she had known when she lived in the house.

The trapdoor under the carpet in the dining

room, which let you down under the house – you could crawl over the rock the house was built on and see the underside of the floors – that was an Alex secret.

Helen and Angelica scared bossy Toby next time he came to stay by disappearing through there completely in a game of hidey.

Then, when he had quite given up and sat down at the dining room table to draw, they scared him even more. They came up under the carpet, almost beneath his feet, groaning horribly.

'Toby, Toby,' they moaned, 'we've come for you, Toby,' but then they began to giggle.

'Just like you stupid girls,' he said, pretending he knew all the time.

'But did you see his face?' said Helen.

Next day they hid behind the waterfall in the creek, where Alex said you could squeeze into a cranny.

Toby was showing off as usual. 'Finding gold is just knowing where to look,' he was saying. Angelica and Helen seemed to be listening for once, so he went on and on. 'Yes, there's gold to be found, but you must know where to look. You'd be wasting your time here.' He had his back to them. Helen nudged Angie and they were gone in a flash.

Toby stopped at last and turned round. There

was no way the girls could have gone past him, or up the rocks by the fall. He called and called, while they hid and laughed. This time he couldn't hear them for the noise of the waterfall. In the end, he gave up and went downstream towards the house.

They rushed out behind him and rolled him in a pool. But they wouldn't tell where they had been.

It was much easier to put up with Toby when there were two people to keep him in order.

But the cave ('quite hidden,' Alex said) they could not find, though she had given directions carefully.

They made an early start, for it promised to be a hot day.

'Above the fall, left,' said Angelica. 'A sort of path, almost grown over, go straight on.'

She had copied out what Alex said, and they hunted about, looking for anything the least like a path, climbing over fallen trees, and getting their faces scratched by bushes.

'A path could disappear in sixty years,' said Angie, 'but she says straight up. And she says to turn left at the bishop rock and that we'd know it at once.'

Higher and higher they went; it was hard going.

'I'm going to sit down and eat my orange,' said Helen. 'We should have brought a drink. The creek seems to have gone down a hole, I can't even hear the fall.'

She peeled the fruit carefully and dropped the peelings in a hole in a tree.

'Now all we want is a little green man to pop out of there and tell us which way to go. Bit of a funny one, your Alex, loves a mystery. Doesn't she say there is something she wouldn't even write about the cave?

'It's like those sets of boxes, all one inside the other. First the diary, then the path, then the rock, then the cave and then you'll find out what.'

She picked a sprig of a prickly wattle and waved it about in front of her face as she talked.

'She was spoilt, Alex, I guess, her mum and Gamma waiting on her hand and foot. Got big ideas about herself.'

'Oh, Helen, don't be horrid. How could you know, anyway?'

'Only child. We're all spoilt. You, me and Alex.'

'You! What about Rob?'

'He's fifteen years older. He doesn't count. He doesn't even *live* in Helicon.

'There probably isn't a cave at all. And if there was, how could you find it in all this tangle?'

'Everything's been right till now, Helen.'

'Oh yes. Third tree on the left past the Post Office. Dig. And you'll find three cans of Coke and a packet of Smarties. Smartie Alex. I'm tired. Let's go home.'

'Helen, you're jealous.'

'Jealous? I guess I am. Your blasted Alex seems more real to you than I am. You never ask *me* anything. I've lived here all my life and you never ask me! For instance, I could tell you why this mountain is called Sailor Bob.'

'Why is it, then?'

'He was a dog. The miners trained him to sniff out gold.'

'Try again, Helen.'

'Well, there was an old fossicker – you know, someone who pokes around looking for gold – he lived in a hut on the mountain. They called him Sailor Bob. He had mermaids and whales and sailing ships tattooed on his arms. Never talked to anyone. Then he disappeared. Found gold and went over the hills to Keeley, they said.'

'Or fell down a cliff?'

'Perhaps. So they called it Sailor Bob's Mountain. Sailor Bob ... We'd better get going again. Sorry, Angie, for blowing off about Alex. But you do go on about her.'

'Maybe I do. But you are the *now* friend, Helen. Alex is different, like something I read in a book.' She felt rather mean as she said it. Alex was as real as Helen, just as Helen had guessed.

As they went on, there began to be rocks among the trees. Sometimes a tree grew right out of one. Sometimes a rock had split into slices like a cake.

'There's your bishop,' said Helen, pointing at a stone as tall as herself, 'but there's another one,' she panted as she scrambled up the hill, 'and another,' she was quite out of breath, 'but they're not red. Sort of pink.'

The trees were much further apart here, you could see the sky between. The sun had gone and dark clouds were rolling up.

'Let's give up,' said Angie, 'it's going to pour. And,' she looked at her watch, 'it's nearly lunch time.'

They went down much faster than they had come up, but even then a shower caught them just before the house and drenched them entirely, so that they had to change. That made lunch later than ever and when it was over it was time to take Helen home.

8
Missing

Things were rather too quiet for a while. The warm weather seemed to have gone, as it often does in October. Days went along like pages turning. It was quiet all day, even quieter at night.

Helen went to Sydney with her mother, Rob was getting married. They stayed away for two weeks.

Dad had to go to Helicon three times to see the dentist, and once Angie stayed overnight with Mrs Wright.

Their farm wasn't very big, but green and

growing. The cows were fat, black and white, the orchard was full of green fruit.

'Cherries come November,' said Mrs Wright. 'Hope the rain doesn't spoil them this year. Maybe it will have rained itself out by then.'

Mr Wright was tall and thin, rather silent. He played the accordion for the local dances.

'That's where I met him, at a dance,' said Mrs Wright. 'He was sat up there, saying nothing to no one, so at supper I went up and had a yarn.'

'And she's been talking ever since,' said Mr Wright, smiling.

'Well, I have to talk for two. I'd go mad waiting for you to tell me anything. So he knows all about you, Angie, even the diary and the cave.'

'The cave we didn't find.'

'I never did hear that there were caves on that mountain,' said Mr Wright. 'Wrong kind of country.'

'Did you ever hear from that Mrs Dalloway?' he went on. 'About the house, I mean.'

'Not yet, Mr Wright.'

'Oh well, old ladies take their time. And it's my time to get the cows in. Want to come with me?'

But it had begun to rain again. 'Drat it,' said Mrs Wright, 'the washing.'

The mountain seemed to be drowned in mist and rain for the whole of October. So when November began hot and bright, they rang Helen, who was back, and said, 'Come on out for the weekend.'

Saturday was fine, but in the evening it began to rain.

'Again!' said Angie. 'It rained nearly all the time you were away.'

'Not to worry,' said Mr Scott, and he got out the big box of games and began to teach Helen how to play Go. They played on and on, the fire crackled, and they made toast with the long old-fashioned toasting fork that had been hanging by the fireplace when they came.

'Quite different from toaster toast,' said Helen. They spread it with forest honey and made cocoa in a saucepan on the coals. Then 'Midnight,' said Mr Scott, surprised. 'Lights out, we'll clean up in the morning.'

In the morning the rain was still pouring down, and the wind howling. Angie switched on the heater as she laid the table for breakfast. It had got very cold for November.

'This looks like going on all day,' said Mr Scott and he turned on the radio to catch the weather. The news was still on.

'... of the six-year-old boy who went missing yesterday afternoon in mountain country near

Helicon. The boy, David Romilly, wandered away from the lookout on Sailor Bob. He was wearing only jeans and jumper when mist came down unexpectedly on the mountain. Overnight the weather has been unusually cold and wet, and further rain is expected. Fog is making the search difficult.'

'That makes *our* wet Sunday look sunny,' said Helen. 'Poor kid. I hope they'll find him soon.'

'They will, don't worry,' said Mr Scott.

But when they took Helen home that night he still had not been found.

The river was almost up to the bridge and the lashing rain heavier than ever. The car slid on the wet road and the windscreen wipers didn't seem to go fast enough. It was hard driving. 'I'll be glad to get home,' said Dad.

When they got in, there were still a few hot coals in the fireplace. Angie stirred them up and put on wood, and soon the fire was roaring up the chimney. It was fun to make a fire. They turned out the light and drank Milo in the firelight. The radio played softly.

'We're cave-dwellers,' said Angelica, 'hiding from the storm. Cave-dwellers with radio.'

'The news!' said her father. 'Let's find out what's happened to the child.'

They listened to the announcer's solemn voice.

'. . . no sign as yet of David Romilly, aged six, missing since Saturday afternoon in the bush north of Helicon. The weather worsened today, with snow on peaks above 1,500 metres.

'Police dogs have been brought in, but without success. It is feared the child, who was not dressed for cold weather, must be suffering badly from exposure.'

Angelica went to the window and looked out into the dark and rain. 'It's so cold out there,' she shivered, 'so wild. Listen to the wind.'

Another wild gust shook the house. 'So dark,' said Angie.

Her father got up and put his arm around her. 'I mean to join in the search tomorrow,' he said. 'For now, let's get to bed. We can't do a thing right now, except hope he's found a dry hole to sleep in.'

She dreamt of Alex that night. Alex was showing her the way to the cave. 'Up past the waterfall, on the left. Straight on till you see the red rock – you'll know because . . .'

She woke up with a start when something went bang on the roof.

Why did she have to wake up just then. Why did she dream of the cave?

'Cave-dwellers' she had said to Dad; perhaps that was it. The cave – if only David had found some place like that.

She didn't go to sleep again for ages. And then Dad was calling her. The room was dim, it was still raining.

He came upstairs. 'Hi, sleepyhead. Still no news, I'm afraid. I've phoned Mrs Wright, she'll be up to stay with you. And our friend Joe, the forestry man, remember?'

'Mmm,' said Angie, sleepily.

'I'm joining his team; blokes like Joe know these mountains like the back of their hands. Don't worry, they'll find him if any one can.'

'You keep telling me that.'

'Yes.' He sighed. 'Well, honey, good-bye, I'm off.'

'If anyone can'. And what if no one could? She lay thinking about it for a while. She thought of Sailor Bob who just 'disappeared'.

Then she sat up suddenly and swung her feet out of bed. She went down to make herself some breakfast; she wanted to finish and clear up before Mrs Wright came so she wouldn't have to stay and talk. She did have work to do.

She tried very hard that morning to settle down to her last assignment for the year. But all she could think of was David lost. And her dream of the cave. She even went up and looked in the diary again, to see if there was anything she had missed, but it didn't tell her anything new. The bishop rock, would that be like a bishop's mitre? Or like a figure in a cloak and tall hat?

In any case, it was red. If she ever found it.

After lunch she sat by the living-room fire. The room was warm and she was sleepy after her broken night. She drifted into a doze. Suddenly she heard Alex's voice again: 'Red rock, turn left.'

She woke with a jump. The rain had almost stopped. She would go out and look. The path might have gone, but the red rock would still be there. She was going to find David.

Into the pocket of her parka she slipped a can of Coke, and a chocolate bar. She said to Mrs Wright, 'I'm going to put on my boots and go up to the waterfall. It must be coming down like Niagara.'

'Niagara!' said Mrs Wright. 'I always wanted to see Niagara. I'll come with you; I can't settle to anything thinking of that child. Wait while I see if a pair of your Dad's boots will fit me.'

The fall, when they got there, was magnificent, white and roaring; you could hear it from the house as soon as you stepped outside.

Angie wished Mrs Wright would go home. 'Up

past the waterfall,' said the diary. 'Go home, Mrs Wright, go home,' she kept saying in her head. But Mrs Wright didn't budge, she was enjoying herself.

Then Spot, who had been poking about and getting himself wet, pricked up his ears and raced up the hill.

'What's he after?' said Mrs Wright, 'Wonder he can hear anything in all this noise.'

Angie whistled, but he didn't come back. 'I think I'll just walk up after Spot,' she said.

'He'll come back. He's just put up a rabbit or something. I'm going back to the house to put on the tea. Come on, I'm getting cold. And these boots leak.

'You've looked before, lovie, if it's that cave you're thinking of. Now don't you go going right up there, we don't want to have to send a search party after *you*.'

'I just want to go a little way,' said Angie, and started up the hill left of the creek.

She took no notice of Mrs Wright's last call: 'Better come back, child . . . Well, I guess the dog's got more sense than you, *he* won't get lost.'

9

What Angelica Found

Angelica kept on up the hill, a bit nearer to the creek than that day with Helen. She could still hear the falls, a distant roar. The forest floor was tangled with fern and low scrub, wet and sweet-smelling.

She came to a place where fallen trees lay uprooted, their butts above her head. She searched for a way round; something – an earthslip? – must have brought them down all at once. Finally she climbed on to a huge trunk by its muddy roots and walked along the trunk to where she could jump down to earth again.

Goodness, was that the time? At this rate she'd not be among the rocks, where surely the cave must be, before dark.

'It's fifty years, Alex,' she said aloud. 'Everything's changed.'

She scrambled up the hill, her jeans soaked, her face stinging where bushes had whipped it. A long scratch on her hand kept bleeding; she'd nothing to mop it with, she licked it clean.

'Straight up'. She couldn't make it, she had to veer left. I'll miss the rock, she thought. Which way now, Alex, which way?

Spot came back from somewhere, wagging his tail, looking into her face. When he found she was going on, he raced way ahead.

She had meant to keep calling as she climbed, but she had forgotten, and wouldn't have had enough breath to spare in any case. But the forest was thinning at last, there were rocks among the trees, it was easier going now.

She stood still a moment and breathed deeply. To the left now?

She gave a long 'Coo ... eeeee.' It only brought Spot back again.

'David,' she shouted. There was only the sound of water dripping, and a bird or two trying its voice after the rain.

A flock of bright parrots, red, green and blue,

63

flashed by, the only living things she'd seen so far. Her eyes flicked about her, as she toiled on upward, looking for a red rock, a cave, anything.

Nothing but trees and tumbled stone, black with wet. Her ears seemed to stretch from their centres like long antennae, trying to catch a voice, a cry.

'Coo ... eeeee!' she called again. 'Da ... vid!'

There was an answering, excited bark from Spot. He seemed to be somewhere above her, to the left.

She climbed, she called, she called, she climbed. And then, faintly, an answering call. She turned towards it, called back, 'Is that you, David?'

Faintly again, an answer. 'Yes! David.'

She whistled to Spot and heard him barking like crazy, but he still didn't come. There seemed to be an open space somewhere to the left; the light was brighter and she saw sky, a patch of blue.

Then she was in a clearing without trees; bare rock glistened and David's voice cried, 'In the cave.'

She saw no cave, only two huge rocks capped by another which had fallen across them. Bushes and a solitary tree grew at their base.

A streak of black and white rushed out of the bushes and danced around her. 'Spot,' she said joyfully, 'where's David, fetch David.'

He tore back into the bushes, she followed, and there, behind, between the rocks, a kind of cave. Huddled against the wall – David.

He was blue and shivering, but he tried a smile. Spot licked his face, wriggling with excitement.

'I knew someone was coming,' he said. 'My ankle hurts. I fell down and it hurts. I can't walk.'

'It's all right now,' said Angelica. 'You'll soon be safe and warm.' She knelt and rubbed his cold hands. She took off her thick jumper and slipped it on him. It came way down to his knees.

She hugged him. 'Soon be home,' she said. 'Let's look at your foot.' His ankle was very swollen.

'I can move it, though,' he said.

'But you can't walk on it? I guess it's sprained.' She sat down beside him and spread her warm, down-filled parka over them both.

'Lunch.' She fished in the pockets. 'Which first?'

'A drink.' His lips were dry. She pulled the tab for him.

'Slowly, then. Now some chocolate.' She broke it into pieces and fed him like a baby. He licked the last trace from round his mouth.

'Nothing for you, Spot. Go home. Fetch. Fetch Mrs Wright.'

He didn't want to go. He ran a little way when

she pushed him, and then came back. Nothing would make him go.

Angie settled David on her lap, her arms round him, the coat covering them both. Spot cuddled against them, she could feel the heat of his small body.

David was still cold, but the shivering stopped as her warmth stole into him. 'Now we've time to talk,' she said. 'I'm Angie, I live down the hill.

'Someone will come for us soon. Mrs Wright, probably.' She smiled to herself thinking of Mrs Wright struggling up here, puffing, and anxious. She must be anxious by now. What was the time? Five o'clock already. She couldn't carry David far in such rough country. She couldn't get down alone much before dark. Best stay here. Someone would come. She would keep calling. And Spot would know if anyone was near long before she would.

'Tell me how you got here, David.'

'It got foggy. I lost the car park. Dad said, "If you get lost ever, go downhill. Follow water."

'I went downhill. I shouted. Once I saw the road, way down. It was foggy, it got dark. I crawled under a rock. I went to sleep.

'When I woke up, it was raining. I went down, a long way. I slipped among the rocks. I couldn't walk properly. Then I found the cave, it was dry and I went to sleep. And today Spot came.'

He was getting sleepy. She called again, Spot barked loudly, David jumped awake.

'There they are, waving. To cheer me up.'

'Who's waving, David?'

'The hands.' He fell sound asleep.

Half-past five. Was that all? Mrs Wright would be sure she was lost, what had she done about it? After a while, she laid David down, still fast asleep, and went outside to call.

'Spot,' she ordered, 'go home.'

He only looked puzzled and whined, dropping his tail. She gave up trying to make him go and went back to David again. He seemed warmer now. The air was warmer too; perhaps it wouldn't matter if they weren't found till morning. But she wished she had put more in her pockets. She was very hungry, and David must be starving.

She became drowsy, holding him on her lap and forgot to call, waking with a jerk when Spot jumped up and rushed from the cave, barking furiously.

She heard an answering bark, the deep voice of a large dog. Men's voices too. And one of them was Dad's.

David woke. 'They're here, David.' She stood up and went to the entrance of the cave.

'Dad,' she cried, 'he's here, David's here. In the cave.'

The men crowded in, pushing back the bushes

at the mouth of the cave. Joe was there. 'A cave,' he said, 'I'd never have known. The kid – how is he? David boy, how's it going?'

'OK, I'm OK. Please take me home. I can't walk, though.'

They looked at his ankle. Sprained, they thought, though you couldn't be sure.

'Piggyback for you, then,' said the third man. But Joe, after a sharp look at the rocky space in front, was already fiddling with his walkie-talkie.

'There's a better way than that,' he said. 'There'll be light enough for a while.' He began to talk to base.

'Fred, where's the helicopter? We've got the kid. East side of Sailor Bob. Above Scott's. Yeah, OK, he's OK ...

'There's a clear space, the chopper can find it, no worries.' He began to give precise directions. 'Tell him ...'

They gave Angie back her parka and wrapped David in a blanket. They gave him a warm drink from a Thermos, Angie too.

'You did a good job, kid,' Joe told her. 'And you, little mate, a tough little guy you are. A real bushman.'

Angie sat and leaned against Dad's shoulder. 'How did you get here so fast?' she asked.

'Mrs Wright got panicky and rang Search and Rescue when you didn't come back. We were near. The dog did the rest.'

The big dog lay quietly, ignoring Spot's cheeky barks and rushes. They waited, not talking, in the gathering dusk.

Then they heard it, the buzz, the uneven drumming of the helicopter. It was circling, answering their waves, hovering just above them. Quickly David was winched aboard, still wearing Angie's jumper, and only one shoe. The helicopter rose, they waved. It was gone. All done so fast.

'Like clockwork,' said Dad. 'Now let's go, we've a long hike back.' They set off downhill, threading the trees and rocks, Joe leading.

An easier way, this, than the one Angie had come, almost a path in fact. 'I know this place,' said Joe, 'but the cave, that's something else. It's not much of a cave, of course, just three big tors. Snug enough to hide him, though.

'Even if it had been clear enough for the chopper, no one could have seen him once he crawled in there.'

'Why did you come up here, Angie?' said her father quietly, as he helped her over a rough spot. 'Was it the diary?'

'Yes . . . And a dream I had. But Spot seemed to know someone was up there. I mightn't have got to the cave without Spot.'

'Thank God it turned out all right,' said her father. 'Poor Mrs Wright was terribly upset. She had half a mind to go looking for you herself.'

The almost path met a real one just as it was getting really dark. They hurried along, Joe and Tom flashing their torches.

Spot went on ahead and was on the doorstep with Mrs Wright when they arrived. The kitchen was cosy, full of delicious smells of soup that simmered on the stove.

'Angie, dear.' Mrs Wright hugged her tight. 'Safe and sound. They rang me from Search and Rescue. I was that glad to hear. And that smart little dog sniffed out the little man.

'You naughty scamp, Angie, going off like that. But all's well that ends well.

'Get those wet dirty things off. Here's your dressing gown and 'jamas, all warm for you. Now get them on . . .

'I guess you're all starving,' she babbled on, excited. 'Joe, Tom, how about some of my soup before you move off?'

Alex, thought Angie. It was Alex really, not Spot or me.

10

The Secret of the Cave

It was days before Angie remembered the secret
Alex had talked about, the secret in the cave.

The weather was dry and warm again, and
Helen was there for the weekend. Nowadays she
seemed to spend nearly every weekend with Angie.

Mr Scott was too busy to take them out this day
– or even to talk to them.

'Keep out, like good girls, do. I've two more
drawings to finish before I send off my book. And
I must catch the mail Tuesday if I can make it.

'Take a picnic up to the waterfall, or something.
Show Helen where you found David.'

It would be a great day for playing under the fall, but Helen was keen to see the cave.

'And I'd forgotten, Helen,' said Angie, 'that Alex said there was a secret in the cave. We hardly looked at it the other day, only David. Let's go there, take our lunch.'

They packed the lunch and started up the hill. It was all different today in the sunshine. They took the track Joe had used and found the almost path which curved off from it, marked with a stone.

'There's your bishop,' said Helen, 'only it's pink, not red.' The oddly shaped granite cone did look something like the chess piece.

'Well, it's not white. You know, in *Alice in Wonderland* the pieces are red and white, not black and white like all I've ever seen.'

'*Alice through the Looking Glass*,' said Helen crushingly. 'And they can be any colour at all. Alex wasn't much on distance, was she. Who would have thought to come this far left of the fall?'

It was certainly a much easier journey than Angie's frantic scramble through the forest had been, not so steep, and the scrub not wet and scratchy. Quite soon they were up among the rocks, and then in the bare rocky space where the helicopter had hovered.

'The mountain shows its bones,' said Helen. 'Where's the cave?'

Above them, the mountain rose in walls and turrets of rock among thin trees.

'Right in front of us. Can't you see it?' said Angie teasingly. 'Come on then, I'll show you. Even Joe didn't know it was there.'

She led the way to where the rounded tors balanced their stony roof. They pushed aside the bushes, rather tattered by now, and went inside.

Helen looked carefully around. Angie expected her to say something sharp about Alex's cave.

What she said was, 'You didn't look at the roof.'

'The roof?' said Angie and looked up.

Then she saw the hands. White hands, a row of them. And little men, dancing.

'Didn't any of you see this the other day?'

'No. Well, I didn't. And the men were only looking at David. It was late and dull, there wasn't much light in here.

'But David talked about hands. I thought he was dreaming.'

'There's something on the wall behind you, though it's almost disappeared. A kangaroo, I think. Red.'

Angie turned round. 'And a huge human. White. Look, there's his head and his left arm. And his feet.'

Helen lay down on her back and studied the roof slab. 'This is fantastic,' she said. 'I'm almost

sure it's a sacred place. There's one near Beech-
worth; our teacher told us about it.'

'Dad will be excited,' said Angie.

'You'll tell him? Why?'

'Well, he'll be interested. And he knows this
professor, Professor Goodfellow, who'll want to
come up and take photographs. Dig, and all that.'

'And what will the black people think about
that?' said Helen. 'Won't they mind? This place
belongs to them. There aren't many places like
this left. Why should white people dig them up?'

'But won't they want to know? The black
people?'

'Alex didn't tell,' said Helen.

No, Alex hadn't told. They were standing outside the cave. The rock stretched before them;
they could see, over tree tops, the plain where
Helicon lay. Beyond that, hills rolled again to the
horizon.

'Think,' said Helen, 'think of them, lots of
people, coming here to meet in this sacred place.
That big white figure in the cave, that's a spirit figure, I expect. And the kangaroo, that makes them
kangaroo people.

'It's a special place, a long time place.'

They sat on the warm rock and looked at the
sky, at its towers and cliffs of white cloud, with their

backs to the rock towers and walls of the mountain.

'Let's not tell, Angie. Perhaps when we find the right person, a black person.

'For now, it's a secret. Yes?'

'A secret,' said Angie.

She suddenly understood what had puzzled her, why Alex had told no one about the paintings, hadn't even written it down. It was not just because she was a girl for secrets. This secret was not really hers.

They went slowly down again, carrying the secret of the cave as if it were heavy. Their secret now!

11

What Happened to Alex

It was hot as midsummer.

Helen, Angie and Toby were sprawled on the lawn under the cedar tree.

'Who is that coming in a horrible pink station wagon?' said Toby.

It was Mr Blackmore and another man. 'Well, young ladies,' he said, 'like my new station wagon? Pink for girls, eh?' Helen was making sick faces at the others.

'Now which of you charming young people will go and tell Mr Scott I'm here?'

Toby rushed off, of course.

Angelica said, 'Mr Blackmore, if you and the other gentleman sit down here in the shade, Helen and I will bring you cool drinks.'

They came back with glasses and a jug of pink drink Mr Scott called 'Persian Princesses' Delight', made of a little yoghurt, rather more raspberry syrup, and a lot of soda.

'Very nice, most unusual,' said Mr Blackmore as he sipped, but he didn't finish it.

And here was Dad,

'Mr Scott, sir,' said Mr Blackmore, 'indeed I'm sorry, but I have a "No" to our last offer. I don't think Mrs Dalloway will ever sell the house. It's not the money, you know, she just loves the place. I'm still trying of course. I've told her what fine tenants you are.'

'A pity,' said Mr Scott. 'I can't spend money on fixing it up if it isn't mine. I want another bathroom for guests, and a bunkroom over the garage. I might even put in a pool.'

'The house is looking good,' said Mr Blackmore, 'more like when she was here. Parties and visitors she used to have. And flowers! Oh my, when I was a boy ...' He stopped.

'Her son will tell her to sell. He never lived here much. She adopted him after ...' he dropped his voice.

The girls tried to look as though they weren't

listening. In fact they listened very hard, but they couldn't hear what he was saying.

Oh dear, thought Angie, we couldn't leave here now, leave Alex. And we promised the Bellamys. And there's Helen. And Mrs Wright.

It was strange that just after that she found out what Mr Blackmore had been whispering about. And all because of Mrs Wright, really.

'I do believe in a really good clean out every so often,' said Mrs Wright. 'I'll do the bedrooms this week, and your little cubbyhole, Angie.'

'I'll do it. It's quite tiny.'

'You can shift everything out for me, lambie, but I'd like to get in there and use a bit of elbow grease myself. We might paint the bookcase and the chair, they're a bit grubby.

'You could do it this very afternoon. There's a couple of boxes in the laundry should be big enough for everything. Run down and get them for me, save my legs.'

After lunch Angie cleared the desk and took the pictures off the wall. Then she began on the books. They *were* dusty. Some of them she hadn't taken out since first she found the room.

She began on the top shelf, dusting as she went down. She remembered her mother doing that.

'Always begin at the top.' She could hear her voice.

Nearly done now. Only the bottom shelf left.

Behind the books was a sheet of paper. Some newspaper cuttings, yellow with age, were fastened to it by a rusty clip.

'Double Tragedy,' said a headline.

'Freak wave drowns two in capsize. Mother watches yacht overturned.'

Her eyes filled with tears, she felt cold and weak. She knew now what had happened to Alex.

She and Gamma, both drowned.

Only Colin saved, clinging to the boat, while Mrs Dalloway, who had watched, who couldn't swim, ran for help.

Angie was crying, bitterly, but she had to know all the story. The rest of the clippings were from other papers, but they said much the same thing.

There was a date pencilled on the top one, 27/1/1931. The date on the sheet of black-edged paper was a month later.

'Darling Alex,' it began,

'I have read your diary, Alex – I am Angelica, too.

'Poor Alex, without a child for company. I didn't guess you minded so much.

'I shall close up your hidey-hole just as it is. I'm going away for a while. Perhaps your Angelica will find the diary one day, who knows.

'Good-bye, little Alex, good-bye.'

Yes. She had guessed it was something like this. The room shut away, all Alex's books in the bookcase.

She cried for a long time. Then she went downstairs, the paper and the clippings in her hand.

'Dad,' she said.

'Why, Angel, what's the matter?'

She couldn't speak. She held the papers out to her father. The sheet of notepaper fluttered to the floor.

'Old-fashioned mourning paper,' he said as he picked it up. Then he was silent as he read. 'Angelica,' he said, 'I'm sorry. I knew about this. Helen's mother told me.'

'And you didn't tell me. Oh, Dad!'

'I thought perhaps Alex would be more real if you believed that somewhere she was alive. I didn't want to make you sad.'

'I think I knew somehow, only I didn't want to know. Perhaps you were right, Dad. Now Alex is really gone.'

'Is anyone really gone, Angel, when we still think of them?'

'Oh Dad, Mum!' she said. 'You are sad for

Mum too.'

She threw herself on him and cried again.

Another letter from America came.

Mrs Dalloway would not sell the house.

Angelica's father looked grim. 'Then we'll move. I'll tell Mr Blackmore to notify her.'

'Move, Dad?' she was horrified. 'Not move!'

'Well, not just now,' he said, 'not just now. But I'm not staying another winter unless ...' He looked at Angelica. 'Angie, you're crying. Does the house mean so much to you?'

'The house,' she said, 'Alex's house. And all the people we've got to know. We can't leave, Dad, we can't.

'She doesn't know, Mrs Dalloway doesn't know that Alex is my friend, that the house likes us.'

'Likes us?'

'Well, it showed us the secret room.'

'Oh, that, well ...'

'We'll write to her. We'll tell her. She might change her mind.'

'It's worth trying,' said her father.

So they wrote a letter. They told her how Angelica had found the diary, how she came to read it. About the good times, about the places

81

Alex had helped her find. About the letter that had fallen out of the diary, and how they'd only just found it. About how they loved the house and that Alex was a friend.

Then they waited for the answer.

12

South to the Lakes

A few days later and 'Angie, what about the Bellamys?' said her father.

'You mean, will I be scared of sailing?'

'Yes.'

'You can't be scared of everything,' said Angie. 'You could stay home for ever.

'You could break your leg falling out of bed; Mrs Wright's mother did,' she added after a moment, seeing her father's look.

'Then we go as planned? And learn to sail?'

'Yes,' said Angie, 'we'll go.'

So they went south, south to the lakes.

It was great to see Andy. And he was on a cloud, he had come third in the Sabot championships.

'Youngest boy in his class,' said Mr Bellamy. 'He'll top them next time.'

To which Andy said nothing, except to ask Angie how soon she could be ready for a sail.

A dreamy holiday. One day almost exactly like another, days of sunshine and bright water. And learning to sail.

It was scary the first time she sailed *Dolphin*. What if she messed it up? But Andy, though he let her do everything herself, was watching, and quietly put her right.

Like the time he said, 'Watch out! She's luffing. Take her off the wind, or she'll be in irons – she won't be able to move. The wind will blow straight past us,' he explained.

And then, 'No, that's too much. We'll bottle. You've got to treat her very gently.'

Bit by bit she got the feel of it, and the scary feeling went away.

Andy didn't talk much when they were sailing, but that didn't matter. All she wanted to do was learn to sail right now. Of course she didn't go out with him every time; there was Sue, and he often sailed alone for practice.

But then she could sail in *Nautilus* and learn

how a bigger boat handled. She could watch Dad taking a lesson from Mr Bellamy. There were picnics to other lakes, and swimming and visits to the entrance to watch the fishermen cross the bar or later unload their catch. Time just flew.

One day, sailing with Andy, he said, 'You're a good crew. When I get a bigger boat, I'd like you on my crew.'

'Are you going to get a bigger boat?'

'Oh yes, someday. And I'm going overseas to sail.' He tossed his hair, bleached almost white by the sun, out of his eyes. 'Someday I'll sail around the world.'

All this seemed very likely to Angie. Andrew was so certain it would happen, it *would* happen.

Sometimes he talked about books, books about sailing and mountain climbing or science fiction. 'Real stuff,' he said. 'Not bug-eyed monsters and space gangsters. Some of their ships could never fly.

'My Dad saw *2,001* sixteen times when he was a kid, and I've seen it three. That was a real spacecraft, that was. They'll do it someday, fly to the stars, and I shall go. I shall be a sky sailor.'

This was something new and strange to Angie. She planned to read some of the books he talked about when she got back home.

Star travel, interplanetary space, all the new and

strange ideas she'd got from Andy were buzzing in her head. That night as they lay on the lawn in the warm dark, the thought of the enormous emptiness between the stars made her shiver. Man to the moon, that was far enough, but to the stars!

'What's the matter, Angel?' said Dad.

'So far away, the stars . . .'

' "Infinite space terrifies me",' he said. 'You are not the only one to feel it. That was said by a famous man long ago.'

'It's just too big,' said Angie. 'I like things smaller.'

'But wonderful,' said her father.

Too soon it was time to leave.

'You must have a boat next year,' said Mr Bellamy. 'I've never seen anyone learn so fast.'

'She's beating me hollow,' said her father.

They said their good-byes, knowing that it wasn't so long till they would meet again, then took the road north through the mountains.

Mile upon mile of winding road, dark tall trees, a narrow ribbon of sky. It got too much for them. They had to stop.

They took a rest from trees and bends beside a little creek which ran over pebbles.

The pebbles were small and of many colours.

They fitted the palm of a hand neatly. To hold them shrank the world again to human size. Instead of huge trees, there were blackberry bushes, the fruit not quite ripe, and weeping willows.

They splashed hot hands and faces with the clear cool water, and spread their lunch out on the bank of the creek.

A tumbling-down house was near by. Young trees were shooting up everywhere; soon no one would know that once there had been a house there at all.

Angelica thought of their house at home. Their house? Would there be a letter from Mrs Dalloway? Would Dad want to move if there wasn't? Move – they couldn't move. The house was home. A place where so many things had happened. A place of friends. The only place in the world where Alex was.

13

The House-Having

Late afternoon they reached Helicon, and called at the Post Office for their mail.

There was a big bundle with a rubber band around it. Dad tossed it on Angie's lap and said, 'Have a look for the airmail ones, could be we'll hear from Mrs Dalloway.'

There was only one airmail from U.S.A., addressed to Mr Scott and Miss Angelica Scott. Sender, Dalloway.

'Read it to me, then,' said Dad. 'We may as well know right away.'

It is hard to open an airletter with your finger,

and Angie looked in the glovebox for something more handy. She came up with a small screwdriver, and got the letter untidily open.

She began shakily, 'Dear Mr Scott and Angelica,' but her voice became joyful as she read the first line:

I have decided to sell you the house. It makes good sense for the house to belong to someone who loves it, to people who will be good to it, and who know my Alex.

My son George says, "Yes, sell it to the Scotts."

I am writing to Mr Blackmore. It can all be fixed up at once. I hope you will be as happy in the house as I once was.

With all good wishes, yours,

Maie Angelica Dalloway.

Angelica jumped for joy. 'The party. You promised. It can be a house-having party too. I wonder how old the house is.'

'Almost a hundred years old.'

'Then it can have a birthday party, a hundredth birthday party.'

Next day they began to make plans.

Lists of people.

Lists of food.

A birthday cake with one hundred candles. Chairs and tables to put on the lawn.

'It's usually fine here in May,' said Mr Scott. 'We'll take a chance.'

Mrs Wright knew someone who would come in and cook. The plans were working out well. They planned an invitation:

> *John Scott and Angelica*
> *invite you to a party on*
> *May 7th, 3.30 to midnight*
> *to celebrate*
> *the birthdays of*
> *John Scott*
> *and ...*

'The house,' said Angelica. 'What's its name?'

'Kelsall Cottage.'

'No. You said we could change.'

'Cosy Cot, Scott Shack, Pine Grange?'

'Those are awful, Dad. Tall Chimneys?'

'So's that. Why not just The House?'

'The White House? The Pines?'

'Not enough pines. I think The White House will do. I hate soppy names for houses.'

So it was The White House.

But they didn't finish the invitations that day – which was just as well.

Just before Easter, a small yellow car stopped at the gate. A woman in a blue dress got out. She stood there, looking.

Just for a moment Angie thought, Mum! But no, she'd know her anywhere. It wasn't Mum.

Angie stood up as the woman came up the path.

'You must be Angelica.' She smiled. 'Could I see your father, please?

'I've got Mrs Dalloway in the car. She'd like to come in and visit for a while.'

Angie jumped with surprise. Mrs Dalloway! What next? She didn't know which way to go first.

She rang the front door bell, which was hardly ever used, and then ran down the path to the car.

'Mrs Dalloway,' she cried. 'Alex's Mum. Dear Mrs Dalloway!'

The old lady got out of the car and put her arms around her.

'Dear Angel,' she said. 'Dear child.'

And there was Dad. 'Come in, come in. Come in out of the heat and tell us how you got here.'

'This is Colin's daughter, Ruth,' said Mrs Dalloway. 'You remember Colin?'

'Of course,' said Angelica. 'Alex's friend.'

'She lives in Wattle Valley. Runs an antique

shop. I'm staying with her just now, just for a little while. But I'm home to stay.

'It was a mistake, going to Atlanta. I missed Australia, I missed my friends. More than I expected.

'George is kind, but they are busy people. No children, but always trips, visits, parties.

'Moving a bit too fast for me, an old lady past eighty.

'So I wrote to Ruth and told her I was coming back. And here I am.'

Angelica had a horrid thought – does she want the house?

But Mrs Dalloway went on, 'We've found a house for me in the town. And a housekeeper.

'Such a nice place, just where the hills begin. Quite fabulous, you might say, Angie. If children still say fabulous.

'I hope you'll often come and visit me.'

'And you must come and visit here whenever you want,' said Mr Scott. 'We've things to tell you.

'Have you heard about Angie's great exploits, how she and Spot, our dog, found a lost child?

'They had their pictures in the paper, were on TV visiting David in the hospital ...'

'The nurses didn't want to let Spot in,' said Mrs Wright, who came in just then with a tray. 'But the TV people were too good for them.

'Mrs Dalloway, is it?' she said, without waiting to be introduced. 'It must feel like old times to you, sitting there on your sofa.'

'Just like older times,' said Mrs Dalloway, looking at Angelica who was hunting in a drawer for the newspaper with the pictures.

'It's a house for a family,' said Mrs Wright.

Angie found the photos. 'There's David,' she said. 'I like best the one with Spot. But you know, Mrs Dalloway, we couldn't have found David if it hadn't been for Alex and her secret cave.'

Mrs Dalloway looked at them carefully. 'Alex,' she said, 'had more than one secret. She was a girl for secrets. Perhaps I can tell you another one.'

'We know the waterfall cave,' said Angie.

'No, not that one. I think I'll keep my secret a little longer, for a dull day sometime.'

Suddenly they all felt hungry. They talked on as they ate Mrs Wright's hot scones with strawberry jam.

There was so much to tell.

It was the morning of the party. The birthday party, the house-having party, the welcome-home-Mrs Dalloway party.

Angie was picking flowers and piling them in the wheelbarrow.

Asters, chrysanthemums, some late roses, arm-
fuls of red leaves and shiny berries.

At last she thought she had enough. It was
going to be a beautiful day. Just perfect for an out-
door party.

She looked at the house, smiling in the morning
sun.

'Mr Scott and Miss Angelica Scott,' she said,
'have much pleasure in inviting you . . .'

She thought of all the friends coming. New
friends, old friends. So many new friends.

She began to count them off on her fingers:

Helen and her mother;

David and all the Romillys, five altogether;

Joe and Tom;

The Bellamys, who should be here any minute,
they were going to stay;

Mrs Dalloway;

Ruth;

Mr and Mrs Wright;

And Alex, best friend.

'It was all because of you, House,' she said.
'Happy Birthday, House, from all of us.'